The Shepherd's Rod 2024

By Bonnie Jones

White Horses Publishing
Pineville, North Carolina

The Shepherd's Rod 2024:
Copyright © 2023 by Bonnie Jones

All rights reserved. No part of this book may be reproduced in any form without written permission from White Horses Publishing.

Unless otherwise noted all Scripture quotations in the publication of the 2024 Shepherd's Rod are taken from the New King James Version. Copyright © 1982 by Thomas Nelson, Inc. Used by permission. All rights reserved.

Also Used - the Amplified® Bible, Copyright © 1954, 1958, 1962, 1964, 1965, 1987 by The Lockman Foundation. Used by permission. (www.Lockman.org)

Printed in the United States of America.

Cover art created by Lyn Kost
(704)-975-9631
lynkost@gmail.com

To obtain more of Bob and Bonnie Jones' written, video and audio teachings, prophecies and materials visit us at
www.BonnieJones.org

or write to: White Horses Publishing
P.O. Box 838
Pineville, N.C. 28134-0838

Acknowledgements

First, I would like to thank Holy Spirit for granting me revelatory dreams and speaking mysteries to my spirit so I can reveal the Father's heart to the body of Christ. I thank the Lord Jesus for granting me wisdom and understanding as He continues teaching me. I also thank Father God for granting me this opportunity to share His love with His children.

Next, I want to thank Bob Jones for introducing me to writing of the Shepherd's Rod. Before his departure to heaven Bob commissioned me with this responsibility. It was Bob's great joy to write the Shepherd's Rod for many years and it continues to be my pleasure.

I want to thank my son Lyn Kost for the outstanding graphic artwork, formatting and final preparation that's made each Shepherd's Rod a success. Each year's cover is consistent with the theme of its' content. Thank you for your diligence and assisting me with the production of this book.

And lastly yet very important, I want to acknowledge my dear friend Marcia Rensink who courageously edits my writing. She most definitely is a picture of long-suffering. She keeps my writing in the right tense and proper form. To her I bequeath a new red ink pen. Thanks Marcia!

My heart is overflowing with a good theme;
I recite my composition concerning the King;
My tongue is the pen of a ready writer. **(Psalm 45:1)**

Introduction to
The Shepherd's Rod

The term "**Shepherd's Rod**" derives its meaning from *Ezekiel 20:37* stating:

*And I shall make you pass under the rod and I shall bring you into the bond of the covenant. **(Ezekiel 20:37)***

For those unfamiliar with the Shepherd's Rod, it is a word from God received around the time of Rosh Hashanah through Yom Kippur which is then released to the Body of Christ some time before the New Year annually. The Day of Atonement (Yom Kippur) is signified in Scripture as one of the most important dates of the Biblical year since the time of Moses. This sacred day continues as a most significant Holy Day even in the present Church age.

For decades Bob Jones received valuable revelations on this day outlining activities of the Holy Spirit for the seasons ahead. These insights have historically proven to be accurate strategic blueprints with spiritual emphasis and preparation. Bonnie Jones and Lyn Kost joined Bob years later and now continue the Shepherd's Rod since his departure.

In application, these words have been used to prepare the body for upcoming blessings from God and potential threats of the enemy. They have also served as a measuring standard for the body to reflect on and grow from. As with the word of God, each individual Shepherd's Rod continues to unfold and bring new meaning with each new year and so never expires as we wait on the Lord. Each new Shepherd's Rod adds to the whole bringing out new dimensions of the heart of God.

Ezekiel 20:37 symbolically portrays a shepherd extending his rod as his sheep pass under the staff for evaluation. In like manner, we as the Lord's sheep, pass under His staff during this season for the same purpose. **Jeremiah 33:13** and **Leviticus 27:32** provide more clarity in this Biblical principle.

In the cities of the mountains, in the cities of the lowland, in the cities of the South, in the land of Benjamin, in the places around Jerusalem, and in the cities of Judah, the flocks shall again pass under the hands of him who counts them,' says the Lord. ***(Jeremiah 33:13)***

And concerning the tithe of the herd or the flock, of whatever passes under the rod, the tenth one shall be holy to the Lord. ***(Leviticus 27:32)***

About the Author

Bonnie Jones is passionate about the love of the Lord and bringing that understanding to the body of Christ. Her desires are to see the body move in unity and learn to love unconditionally. She encourages the body to hear the voice of God and obey what they hear. She's strong on the "spoken word" and believes that you live with the consequences of the choices you make, so choose wisely! She is a real stickler for truth therefore she carries a strong mantle of justice. Her ministry is full of laughter that breaks the yoke of religion and sets people free to receive the love of the Lord. She also has a great love for children of all ages and speaks into their destinies.

Bonnie continues to walk in the same type of anointing as her late husband Bob Jones did and carries on his mandate to ask the body "Did you learn to love?" In 2021, she founded the "Daughters of the Dawn" Ministry. Daughters of the Dawn is called to be an army of women according to Psalm 68:11 (AMPC) because, The Lord gives the word [of power]; the women who bear and publish [the news] are a great host. Therefore, this ministry is called to equip and release women to move into their anointing through humility and love.

Bonnie has a son, Lyn Kost (Katie), a daughter Kimberly Glover (Doug) and seven grandchildren, Mychal, Brandon, Jordon, Olivia, Avalyn, Sophia, and Ephraim. She walks in a measure of faith and wisdom, speaking life into everyone she meets. She spreads joy everywhere she goes. For the joy of the Lord is her strength! (Nehemiah 8:10)

TABLE OF CONTENTS

	Acknowledgements	3
	Introduction to the Shepherd's Rod	4
	About the Author	6
	Forward	8
1	Awaken The Bride To First Love	12
2	The Remnant Transcends Time	23
3	Year of Open Doors of Opportunity	37
4	Year of the Woman	53
5	No Trespassing	69
	Summary	80

Forward

A Word for America
And the Church

This past year has been one of the strangest yet most blessed seasons I've experienced. The body of Christ has been in a time of transition. It's like the whole body has been in a whirlwind and God is transitioning people quickly. He's moving them where they need to be for His purpose. Many times, we can't understand the "why" or the "where" or even the "timing." But I do know this; we must have an ear to hear and when He says go, we must follow the cloud.

He is repositioning Himself for our benefit. Like Moses and the Red Sea, He positioned Himself between the children of Israel and Pharaoh. And that's what He's doing with His children today. Things that have been opposing the anointing are being moved out of the way so the body of Christ can move forward. There are no more delays!

It's time for the body of Christ to take hold of the helm of this ship and guide it through the rough waters to dry ground. There is nothing the body lacks except confidence. We must have faith in God and not let our mind deceive us. Christ is the anchor of our hope not our economy. We must trust Him in all things.

[Now] we have this [hope] as a sure and steadfast anchor of the soul [it cannot slip and it cannot break down under whoever steps out upon it—a hope] that reaches farther and enters into [the very certainty of the Presence] within the veil, Where Jesus

has entered in for us [in advance], a Forerunner having become a High Priest forever after the order (with the rank) of Melchizedek. ***(Hebrews 6:19-20 AMPC)***

There is a crisis coming but for those who hear God's voice and prepare themselves in Him, they will not have long term effects like those who don't. This is where the rubber meets the road. His children must be willing to lend to others. Or will they hoard everything for themselves?

Vision - When the Lord spoke this to me, I saw people waiting in long lines to get food. It reminded me of old film footage from the 1930's after the Stock Market crash of 29. On a positive note, there was no looting or violence, only people waiting in very long lines.

It's time for the American church to wake up, turn their back to sin, and open their heart to the Gospel. The church can no longer compromise the Word of God. The plumbline is already in place and angels are harvesting the fields. (Matthew 13:41-42) But many in the body are not ready. Mainline churches need to adhere to the whole Gospel before God permanently closes their doors.

The Son of Man will send out His angels, and they will gather out of His kingdom all things that offend, and those who practice lawlessness, and will cast them into the furnace of fire. ***(Matthew 13:41-42)***

There is an economic decline coming and the road will be bumpy. America and the rest of the world shall go through an economic decline, but God will help His people maneuver through this difficult time. They must love and trust Him and He will set a table before His children in the presence of their enemies. And their cup of anointing shall overflow and bring healing to others in distress.

You prepare a table before me in the presence of my enemies; You anoint my head with oil; My cup runs over. **(Psalm 23:5)**

The Shepherd's Rod

2024

1

It is time for the remnant to grasp hold of this sword and deliver the charge it has been given.

Awaken the Bride to First Love

This dream takes place in the Baptist Church where I attended when I was young. I was either engaged or married to another man. Shiny gold buttons on the sleeve of a soldier caught my eye as I glanced across the sanctuary. He was standing at the back of the sanctuary but just then turned so I could see his face. It was my first love, a tall handsome marine wearing his dress Blues. My heart was beating rapidly as I ran toward him. Once I spotted him, I couldn't see anything else and nothing else mattered. I wanted to be in his embrace. As I ran to greet him thoughts flooded my mind. I was surprised to see him at the Baptist Church. In fact, I thought, he doesn't go to church, what's he doing here? Perhaps he's come looking for me? I continued moving toward him, never taking my eyes off him. He's been gone so long, and I've missed him so much, but now he's returned to me. He is my beloved and I am his. I must be embraced by my first love. His eyes were full of love as he gazed down at my face and pulled me near him. This was my one true love. (End of dream.)

I believe this dream symbolizes the Lord wooing the church. Over the years a religious spirit moved into the church replacing Holy Spirit. Many churches worldwide still do not embrace Holy Spirit. This spirit replaced the gifts of the Spirit that God intended His body to use as tools to equip the saints for ministry. According to 1 Corinthians 12:4-9, the nine gifts are wisdom, knowledge, faith, gifts of healings, working of miracles, prophecy, discerning of spirits, tongues and interpretation of tongues. The Holy Spirit is a gentleman, and He will not go where He's not welcome. Unfortunately, many churches closed the door to the gifts and settled for programs initiated by man instead of the power of God.

Over the years the church at large dealt with the religious spirit and many church bodies overcame it. Where the religious spirit bred division, Holy Spirit brought unity to those who embraced Him. I believe there's been a great move of the Holy Spirit in denominational churches in the last 20 years. This dream indicates the body of Christ is ready to receive her first Love, the Lord Jesus Christ. The veil of deception was removed from the bride's mind and replaced with the Spirit of Truth.

Notice what happened, in this dream I represent the beloved who abandoned everything at once and ran to be with her first love. And that is what the Bride of Christ is doing today. He is all that truly matters to her, He is her only focus. Her fiancée or husband represents the carnal nature or world' system that she quickly abandons to be with her Beloved, the Lord Jesus.

Marine Corps Dress Blues and Symbols

The Emblem – Eagle, Globe, Anchor

I want to take a brief look at the Marine Corps Dress Blues. Their emblem is a gold eagle, a globe, and an anchor. It represents the proud nation it defends, America. This emblem is found on 4 places on the uniform. One on the center of the cover, one on each side of the high collar, and one on the belt buckle of enlisted marines above rank of corporal.

The "eagle" represents America, and it stands ready with our coastlands in sight of the entire world. The entire world is within reach of its outstretched wings. The "globe" represents our worldwide presence, impact, and reputation as a fighting force that wins on behalf of our nation's people and progress. The "anchor" points both to the Marine Corps' naval heritage and its ability to access any battleground across any coastline in the world. Together, the eagle, globe, and anchor symbolize America's commitment to defend our nation and advance its ideals.

Eagle - Prophetically eagles represent prophets because some prophets are known as seers and an eagle's vision is far superior to man's. Eagles have a highly developed sense of sight which allows them to easily spot prey. Eagles can see things from 20 feet away that we can only see from 5 feet away. Eagles have a 340-degree visual field that allows for both excellent peripheral and binocular vision. An eagle in flight can reputedly sight a rabbit two miles away. In comparison, a prophet sees well into the future beyond what man can see with the naked eye Abraham saw the life of the coming Messiah some 1900 years before Christ was born.

*Jesus said, "Your father Abraham rejoiced to see My day, and he saw it and was glad." **(John 8:56)***

Comparatively speaking, eagles (the prophets) soar higher than any other bird. They have the ability to go above the snake line. So, what is the snake line? It's a demon-free zone. It's the place the enemy cannot go because the prophet enters the presence of God and Satan does not have permission to enter. Therefore, the prophet comes into the presence of God to receive revelation for the body of Christ and reveal it to those who have an ear to hear.

Here is an excerpt from Bob Jones' book "Above the Snake Line."

This is what the Angel of Truth had told me. He was going to go forth working and preparing for this time. And that we would be above the snake line. Well, what is above the snake line? How do you get there? Above the snake line, it's above the demon line. Much of the church is believing for a cancer free zone. There is a demon free zone. For there is no unclean spirit that will be there. And the way to get there is Isaiah 35, the Highway of Holiness.

(End of Excerpt)
(This experience took place in 1993.)

Globe - The last words Jesus spoke before he ascended commissions all believers to take the gospel throughout the entire world. I believe the globe on this emblem symbolizes the gospel going to the ends of the earth. The eagle's outstretched wings guiding its direction by the Holy Spirit.

And He said to them, "Go into all the world and preach the gospel to every creature. He who believes and is baptized will be saved; but he who does not believe will be condemned. And these signs will follow those who believe: In My name they will cast out demons; they will speak with new tongues; they will take up serpents; and if they drink anything deadly, it will by no means hurt them; they will lay hands on the sick, and they will recover."

So then, after the Lord had spoken to them, He was received up into heaven, and sat down at the right hand of God. And they went out and preached everywhere, the Lord working with them and confirming the word through the accompanying signs. Amen. **(Mark 16:15-20)**

Anchor - The anchor symbolizes our anchor of hope. The apostle Paul tells us that as believers God will fill us with joy and peace. Not just that we will have hope but that we will abound in hope. (Romans 15:13). The power of the Holy Spirit fills us with joy and peace and our hope abounds. (Hebrews 6:11). Our abounding hope is in Christ and eternal life is the anchor of our soul that keeps us steady and calm through all the storms of adversity in life. I like how the Amplified Classic version describes this verse, it says, *"[Now] we have this [hope] as a sure and steadfast anchor of the soul [it cannot slip, and it cannot break down under whoever steps out upon it a hope] that reaches farther and enters into [the very certainty of the Presence] within the veil."*

Gold Buttons - The gold buttons worn on USMC Dress Blue Jackets feature an eagle perched atop and anchor with 13 – 5-point style stars evenly spaced out across the button's upper half. Originally, they were six-point stars, but a five point is used today. Three on each sleeve and 7 on the front of the jacket from waist to neck.

A button is used to secure an article such as clothing and is used as a fastener by passing it through a buttonhole or loop. Here I believe it is saying, "the prophet of our life Jesus Christ is seated atop the anchor of our soul. 13 represents the apostolic (Paul being the 13th apostle) and 5 represents grace. I believe we are in the season and timing when the apostolic is restored to its position of governmental authority. This gold button fastens the prophetic and apostolic together bringing forth the glory of God by direction of Holy Spirit. Prophetically we have moved beyond the work of man's labor (6) into the grace of God's favor (5).

The Blood Stripe – White Gloves – Cover – Belt - The legendary blood stripe is worn on dress blue trousers today symbolizing honor and our nation's eternal gratitude for all fallen marines. A marine's white gloves indicate integrity and discipline. And their **cover** represents the pride and professionalism of the Marine Corps. Only Commissioned Officers are permitted to wear white belts. Prophetically the midnight blue jacket speaks of deep revelatory gifts and the blood stripe on the trousers represents the blood of Christ shed for all mankind that believers are called to walk in. White gloves represent purity and clean hands, (Psalm 24:4) the believer's mind should always be covered in the holiness of Christ, (1 Corinthians 2:16) and keeping the belt of truth always tightened. (Ephesians 6:14)

The Mameluke Sword - A marine's uniform is not complete without the sword. The Marine Corps Dress Blue uniform includes a Mameluke Sword named after the Mameluke Chieftain in North Africa who gave his sword to Lt. Presley O'Bannon in 1805. O'Bannon and his marines marched 600 miles of the North African desert to rid the shores of Tripoli of pirates and rescue the kidnapped crew of the USS Philadelphia. By 1825, all marine officers carried the Mameluke Sword in recognition of this historic battle and the Marine Corps' first victory on foreign soil. This sword is the oldest weapon still in service in the United States armed forces. Today only Commissioned Officers carry the Mameluke Sword.

The remnant has been commissioned through the power of the living Word of God. A Commission is authority, it's given to someone who is officially charged to perform a task or certain duties. Jesus gave His disciples the "Great Commission" and sent them out to perform it. That Commission has never ceased. Too many Christians have felt insignificant and unable to perform the Great Commission, but God has empowered His believers to do so. It is time for the remnant to grasp hold of this sword and deliver the charge it has been given.

*And Jesus came and spoke to them, saying, "All authority has been given to Me in heaven and on earth. Go therefore and make disciples of all the nations, baptizing them in the name of the Father and of the Son and of the Holy Spirit, teaching them to observe all things that I have commanded you; and lo, I am with you always, even to the end of the age." **(Matthew 28:18-20)***

Shoes/Boots - Let us not forget the bold black polished shoes/boots of a proud marine. Boot polishing is the pride and joy of all marines. Some basics are necessary like removing shoelaces, dust, and dirt from the shoe to begin the process. Using a cotton ball with a small amount of water is necessary to apply the polish. It's applied in a circular motion then buffed with a soft cloth. This process is repeated until they get a high shine like a mirror. Because the marine has created a new mirror or glass like surface that reflects whatever is put in front of it. The main key here is patience because it may take 20 to 30 coats to get a high gloss shine. A mirror shine on the marine's boots requires a certain level of discipline and is easily noticeable to their Unit Commander.

Prophetically, like a marine in full Dress Blues, Christians are dressed in the full armor of God. Ephesians 6:11-18 gives us full details of our dress code. In a marine's preparation of boot polishing, they first need to remove any dust, dirt, and obstructions before they begin. They start by removing shoelaces. In the same way Christians are delivered from hindrances after salvation. Shoelaces always speak to me of bridling the tongue. (James 1:26) Shoelaces hold the tongue of the boot in place and Christians need to use wisdom in their speech. As we allow Holy Spirit to cleanse and purify us, we begin to shine with the glory of the Lord. 1 Corinthians 13:12a says that we see in a mirror, dimly, but then face to face, drawing nearer to the Lord as each layer is removed. The Lord uses a gentle touch to cleanse our rough edges.

Like the marine, we must be patient because there are often many layers of wounds that need to be removed. And with each level of deliverance, we begin to shine like a mirror with unveiled face beholding as in a mirror the glory of the Lord. (2Corinthians 3:18) We're continuously being refined, restored, and renewed into the new creation in Christ (2 Corinthians 5:17) as we take on His divine nature. (2 Peter 1:4) Then we can stand against the wiles of the enemy with our feet shod in the gospel of peace. It takes a lot of discipline but our Commander in Chief takes notice.

But we all, with unveiled face, beholding as in a mirror the glory of the Lord, are being transformed into the same image from glory to glory, just as by the Spirit of the Lord. **(2 Corinthians 3:18)**

Semper Fidelis - Semper Fidelis is the motto of the Marine Corps, and it means "Always Faithful" in Latin. It's always being faithful to the country and always faithful to the Corps. Marines are also loyal to their brothers and watch their backs, helping whenever necessary. The trust and the morale marines carry within themselves is not something that's given, it's something that's developed and carried inside them. Marines are proud to pick up the torch and step into the boots of the people that laid the groundwork for this great country, those who fought and died to keep America where it is.

Prophetically, I believe the remnant being commissioned today has a higher calling. They are and must remain faithful to the Lord Jesus Christ and His cross without compromise. They've been commissioned by the sword of the Lord to release power from on high as it has been endued to them. They are always faithful to the Kingdom of God and carry forward the anointing of the great cloud of witnesses from past generations.

Abraham, Moses, David, Elijah, Elisha, Peter, Paul, and John's lives are not complete without us. Hebrews 11:39-40 says that their testimony is not made perfect apart from us. Martin Luther, John Wesley, George Whitefield, Smith Wigglesworth, John G. Lake, Kathryn Kuhlman, Bob Jones, Billy Graham all walked in a measure of past anointings. Now the remnant will continue to walk in a greater measure of power until their testimony is complete. We, like them, are picking up the torch and stepping into the boots of past saints that laid the groundwork for the anointing of the fiery sword being released today.

I'm always amazed how the Lord uses different people in my dreams to represent something significant that I can relate to. Sometimes my sister represents Wisdom (Proverbs 7:4) and sometimes my mother represents the church. Often, I represent the bride and Bob the Holy Spirit, while my first husband can represent the Father. After all he is the father to my children. So just in case you're wondering, my first boyfriend joined the Marine Corps right out of high school. Over the years he's showed up a couple times in my dreams always wearing his Dress Blues. Instinctively I know he represents the Lord as my first love. That's why in this dream I was so excited to see Him and abandoned everything else to be with Him. As a young teenager I didn't know anything about love except my love for family, however, I liked this young man a lot. He left home for the boot camp, just one of the boys from the neighborhood. However, after 13 weeks he came home on leave before deploying for Vietnam. He was a proud and handsome marine, and I didn't even recognize him. Oh yes, both my husbands were marines, so I feel like I've served two tours of duty. And you know what they say, "Once a marine always a marine!" That's the way of the Corps. Semper Fi!

2

Why is Your apparel red, and Your garments like one who treads in the winepress?

The Remnant Transcends Time

Qualifications for Commissioning

Several days following the dream about the bride and her first love, I had an extraordinary experience. I saw the Lord reach down from heaven with a fiery sword in His hand. A marine wearing his dress blues reached out with both hands and the Lord placed the sword across his white gloves. As He did, power was released through the sword, and the fire of God was its power. Immediately the power of the fiery sword transformed and transfigured the marine to transcend through time. This power will transcend its recipient through time to distribute power to other believers. When I came out of this experience, I heard the first stanza of The Battle Hymn of the Republic.

The Mameluke Sword is "only" given to Commissioned Officers in the Marine Corps. Therefore, they carry the sword while wearing the Dress Blues. It's a vital part of the uniform and not complete without it. I believe this experience indicates the commissioning of the remnant this Day of Atonement. They have been commissioned to release the fire of God in power.

Every past generation produced a remnant who would impart to the next one. These walked in obedience to God never compromising the work of the cross. They walked the road less traveled known as the Highway of Holiness of Isaiah 35. Despite persecution and attacks of the enemy they walked by faith not by sight trusting God regardless of circumstance. The remnant marched fearlessly through the trenches quenching the fiery darts of the enemy. They stood for justice and truth while proclaiming victory over Satan. They remained fearless warriors that never cowered in the face of battle. They're the intercessors who stood in the gap for the innocent, the widow and orphan. They never gave up and never gave in.

This remnant has been transformed into the divine nature of Christ Jesus and transfigured by His glorious light flowing through them. Each test, trial, and tribulation prepared and qualified them for commissioning. They faced each battle head on and how they handled it determined their position of commissioning. They learned valuable lessons from the mistakes of past generations. Ecclesiastes 3:15 says, "That which is has already been and what is to be has already been; and God requires an account for what is past." Therefore, the ones being commissioned today will not take the glory for themselves. As the power of God works through them, they immediately give God all the honor and glory. They clearly understand they're only empty vessels God is using to display His power. This remnant remains humble and teachable with their ear to the heart of the Lord, ready and always available for His service. They carry forth the great commission and release other believers to carry it forward in power.

And as you go, preach, saying, "The kingdom of heaven is at hand. Heal the sick, cleanse the lepers, raise the dead, cast out demons. Freely you have received, freely give." **(Matthew 10:7-8)**

Transcending Through Time

The remnant will transcend through time then they'll distribute the power of the sword to other believers. So, what is it and how does this happen? Webster says to transcend is to rise above or go beyond the limits of, to triumph over the negative or restrictive aspects of. It is to be prior to, beyond, and above (the universe or material existence) and to rise above or extend notably beyond ordinary limits.

Let me challenge your thinking for a moment. I believe God is talking about living in and operating from the eternal realm. God is eternal and we were made in His image. (Genesis 1:26). When we were born again, we were born into the Kingdom of God. However, we live on the earth and are bound by the limits of time. But I believe that now we are going to begin operating from the eternal realm.

Let's look at some Scripture. In Matthew chapter 14 we have two good examples. First, 5,000 plus people are gathered to hear Jesus' sermon. The only food available is 5 loaves of bread and 2 fish. Looking up to heaven, He blessed and broke and gave the loaves to the disciples: and the disciples fed the multitudes. Jesus transcended the time (the earthly realm) and accessed the eternal realm. He brought the quantity and quality of heaven to earth through the spoken word when He blessed it. (Matthew 14:14-21)

In the same way God spoke from eternity and created all things when He said, "Let there be!" Let is a verb that means to permit or allow, and it must take action. Each time God said "let" something happened - light, water, fruitfulness, and mankind. (Genesis 1:3, 6, 9, 11, 14, 20 & 24)

Look what happened next. Jesus told His disciples to get in the boat and go to the other side He would join them later. Then He sent the multitudes away. But the disciples boat encountered a storm, the waves were tossing them about, and the wind was contrary. (vs 22-24)

Now in the fourth watch of the night Jesus went to them, walking on the sea. And when the disciples saw Him walking on the sea, they were troubled, saying, "It is a ghost!" And they cried out for fear. But immediately Jesus spoke to them, saying, "Be of good cheer! It is I; do not be afraid." **(vs 25-27)**

Here again Jesus transcended time and walked on water. Peter challenged the Lord, he said, "Lord, if it is You, command me to come to You on the water." And the Lord said, "Come." And when Peter had come down out of the boat, he walked on the water to go to Jesus. At this point Peter stepped out of time and into the eternal realm. He walked on water and went toward Jesus. Yet when he saw the severity of the storm, he was afraid and began to sink. I've heard it said that Peter lost faith because he took his eyes off Jesus, and I believe that is true. Yet I believe he accessed eternity momentarily until fear gripped his soul. Then he cried out to the Lord, "Save me!" And the Lord rebuked Peter's lack of faith and doubt. (vs 28-31)

Other examples of Jesus transcending time are each time He raised the dead. The little girl in Matthew 9:23-25. People said she was dead, but Jesus said she was only sleeping. He stepped into that eternal realm transcending time and brought her out from the sleep of death into life. And the widow of Nain's son was dead and, in a casket, as they were carrying it through the street. In her grief and Jesus' compassion He transcended time and delivered her son back to life. (Luke 7:14-15) I believe Elijah (1 Kings 17) and Elisha (2 Kings 4) had the same type of experiences when they raised the dead to life. They were a type and shadow of things to come.

Then He came and touched the open coffin, and those who carried him stood still. And He said, "Young man, I say to you, arise." So, he who was dead sat up and began to speak. And He presented him to his mother. **(Luke 7:14-15)**

In my experience, I saw a timeline as the sword was placed on the marine's white gloves. There was a supernatural light with power coming through the sword and the marine transcended through time to eternity. The marine, who represents the remnant, went through a portal of time in a twinkling of an eye, yet he never moved a muscle. I believe this remnant will be allowed to access the eternal realm through a portal of time. And in obedience to the Father, they'll be commissioned to change or modify certain things. Now I'm not talking about new age beliefs and practices. I'm saying, "The remnant will be on specific assignments for the Lord." This has nothing to do with them, in fact much of what they'll do will be done in secret. This is for His glory not them but what they do will affect many. I believe the remnant is like Christ's inner circle of disciples. He called 12 to follow Him, then selected 3 to draw near. Peter, James, and John remained close to Him on many occasions when He performed miracles such as raising the dead. And these three had the greatest ministries after He ascended.

The Fiery Sword

The first time "sword" is mentioned in Scripture is Genesis 3 when God drove man out of the Garden. After Adam's disobedience, God could not permit him to partake of the tree of life. It seems access to this tree would have prolonged Adam's physical life indefinitely, dooming him to an eternity in a cursed world. Therefore, God had to prevent

Adam's access to the tree of life by placing cherubim with a flaming sword to guard it.

So, He drove out the man; and He placed at the east of the Garden of Eden the cherubim and a "flaming sword" which turned every way, to keep and guard the way to the tree of life. ***(Genesis 3:24)***

David

Throughout Scripture the sword has been significant. David was a fearless shepherd boy who had already killed a lion and a bear while keeping his sheep safe. While the whole Israelite army feared Goliath, David was unafraid. David knew he was anointed by God and would one day rule as king. (1 Samuel 16:12-13) I believe this gave him an added measure of faith knowing God was with him. Saul blessed David and then dressed him in his armor, a bronze helmet and coat of mail (scales). But when David fastened Saul's sword to the armor, he couldn't walk. (1 Samuel 17:38-39) You see you must walk in your own anointing, not try to imitate another man's. Saul stood head and shoulders above other men and David was just a lad. David removed Saul's armor and picked up his shepherd's staff and gathered 5 smooth stones. David ran toward the army to meet the uncircumcised Philistine and slew Goliath with one smooth stone. However, David used Goliath's sword to remove his head. The Lord provided the enemy's sword to complete David's victory. If He is for us, who can be against us? (Romans 8:31)

David prevailed over the Philistine with a sling and a stone and struck the Philistine and killed him. But there was no sword in the hand of David. Therefore, David ran and stood over the

Philistine, took his sword, and drew it out of its sheath and killed him, and cut off his head with it. (1 Samuel 17:50-51)

Joshua

Joshua led the second generation of the children of Israel over the Jordan River. You could say this was the remnant. The first generation died in the wilderness because of their disobedience to God. But none of this generation were circumcised and could not proceed to Jericho until they were. Joshua made a flint knife and circumcised all the men. Then he had an encounter with the Commander of the Army of the Lord. Of course, at first Joshua did not recognize Him. He only saw a man standing with His sword drawn. Being curious as to the man's motive, he asked, "Are You for us or for our adversaries?" Joshua was a warrior and would have welcomed the challenge. To his surprise the man answered, "No, but as Commander of the army of the LORD!" Then Joshua was instructed to take off his sandals because the place where he stood was holy ground.

And it came to pass, when Joshua was by Jericho, that he lifted his eyes and looked, and behold, a Man stood opposite him with His sword drawn in His hand. And Joshua went to Him and said to Him, "Are You for us or for our adversaries?" So He said, "No, but as Commander of the army of the Lord I have now come. And Joshua fell on his face to the earth and worshiped, and said to Him, "What does my Lord say to His servant?" (Joshua 5:13-15)

I believe the fiery sword today's remnant receives is measured by the holiness of God they possess. The remnant lives according to the Highway of Holiness. (Isaiah 35) Bob would call it the Higher Way in Christ because they are called to a higher standard and greater measure of accountability in Christ. Therefore, like Joshua more is expected from the remnant. And that is why they will transcend time to deliver whatever is necessary to other believers.

Gideon's Sword

Here again we see a remnant that God used for His glory. Gideon started out with an army of 32,000 men, but the Lord kept narrowing it down until there were only 300 men left. A small remnant is all God needed. Their weapons consisted of a trumpet, an empty pitcher, and a torch. Gideon knew the plan of the enemy and knew the battle was already won before it began. His 300 men were divided into 3 groups of 100 each. When he gave the signal, they charged forward declaring, "The sword of the Lord and of Gideon!" Their enemy possessed swords, however the fear of Gideon's mighty men of valor frightened them. When the 300 blew their trumpets, the Lord set every man's sword against his companion throughout the whole camp and the army fled. (Judges 7:22)

Battle Hymn of the Republic

When I came out of this experience, I heard the first stanza of "The Battle Hymn of the Republic" and I knew it was referring to Isaiah 63.

Battle Hymn of the Republic Lyrics

Mine eyes have seen the glory of the coming of the Lord
He is trampling out the vintage where the grapes of wrath are stored
He has loosed the fateful lightening of His terrible swift sword
His truth is marching on.

Glory, glory Hallelujah
Glory, glory Hallelujah
Glory, glory Hallelujah
His truth is marching on

In Isaiah 63 the prophet sees a man and His garments are stained as if He's been in the wine press. But then Isaiah realizes it's the Lord of Hosts. And the Lord explains that He is the God of Justice and Righteousness unto Salvation. And He's going to fight all enemies of Israel. He's wearing a white robe yet He's coming as the Warrior King. It's a supernatural battle and He's not ashamed of the blood He has spilled. Because every enemy of Israel is an enemy of God. And God is going to bring about Justice. He's trampling down the vintage where the grapes of wrath are stored.

Why is Your apparel red, And Your garments like one who treads in the winepress? "I have trodden the winepress alone, and from the peoples no one was with Me. For I have trodden them in My anger and trampled them in My fury; Their blood is sprinkled upon My garments, And I have stained all My robes. For the day of vengeance is in My heart, And the year of My redeemed has come. I looked, but there was no one to help, and I wondered that there was no one to uphold; Therefore, My own arm brought salvation for Me; And My own fury, it sustained Me. I have trodden down the peoples in My anger, Made them drunk in My fury, And brought down their strength to the earth." (Isaiah 63:2-6)

Bob Jones' Visitation

I feel it's important to share some experiences Bob Jones had long ago. A visitation from the Lord in 1984 and the second one was in the mid 90's, another from 2011. I believe they're significant today because it's a time these prophecies are being fulfilled. Many times, when the Lord reveals His secrets, they aren't for the current day but for a future time. We are now entering into a prophetic season where the bride is awakened to her rightful place. And as you read Bob's experiences you will agree that the Tabernacle of David is being restored, the dread champions are arising, and power is once again returning to the church.

Bob's experience July 3, 1984

In the Spring of 1984, an angel came to Bob and told him the Lord was going to visit him that year on July 3rd. Bob set that day aside and waited on his screened in porch for the Lord to come. At 3:00 that afternoon the Lord Jesus came to him in a white light and sat down at the table next to Bob. He said, "Dear friend, I've waited a long time for this visit." Then He asked Bob if he had any questions he wanted to ask. Bob had thought all day about things he would like to ask the Lord however he felt it was more important that he listened to what Jesus had to say. The Lord told him about many things that would take place in the future.

One thing the Lord told Bob was that the "Tabernacle of David" was being restored to 24/7 worship. He said it fell because people took the glory for themselves, they used it wrongly causing a breach. When David's Tabernacle is restored, the glory will be given to Him, so it abides.

On that day I will raise up the Tabernacle of David which has fallen down and repair its damages; I will raise up its ruins and rebuild it as in the days of old. ***(Amos 9:11)***

Jesus visited with Bob for 30 minutes and then He asked Bob to pray three things back to Him. The first prayer was

Psalms 12:1, "Help Lord for the godly man perishes and no one takes it to heart." The Lord told Bob how David and his mighty men of valor were "Dread Champions." And these dread champions are rising now and going throughout the whole world. Dread Champions are ones who are not afraid to live for Jesus. Dying for Jesus is easy but living for Him is difficult. They are willing to live for Him uncompromisingly amid every storm of adversity. Living according to the Word of God when all circumstances are against them.

The second prayer Bob was asked to pray is that Christians' faith fails not. For gross darkness is coming upon the face of the earth and even Christian's faith will fail. Bob prayed, "Lord, help the church to overcome unbelief." The Lord told Bob that he must build faith in believers – the God kind of faith – knowing who they are in Christ and who Christ is in them.

And the third prayer - Jesus told Bob to pray and ask Him to give us power! This glorious power belongs to us – the body of Christ. "Behold, I give unto you power." (Luke 10:19) and "All power is given unto me." (Matthew 28:18) When Bob had finished praying these three prayers to the Lord, Jesus said that He was doing them in the order Bob prayed.

1) Restore the Tabernacle of David to 24/7 worship, raise up dread champions,
2) Maintain faith among the believers,
3) Give the body of Christ power.

Excalibur

Years ago, in a vision, Bob Jones saw the Legend of King Arthur and him pulling the sword from the stone. Bob said this was the "Excalibur" being pulled from the Rock of Ages. It's the Sword of the Spirit and the Word is now more powerful than ever before. Because true believers are walking in power and glory.

Today's remnant possesses a fiery two-edged sword that transcends through time to accomplish what the Lord sends it to do. This sword is His power and might by His Spirit. It's the power of the spoken word, it's the might of the sword.

Finally, my brethren, be strong in the Lord and in the power of His might. Put on the whole armor of God, that you may be able to stand against the wiles of the devil. **(Ephesians 6:10-11)**

Mystic Forces

In 2011 Bob saw 4 beings loosed on the earth. He said these are the four horns from Zechariah 1:18-19. Bob saw these mystic forces as a deer, cat, boar hog and giant or dragon. He said these are principalities, powers, thrones, and dominions. And he gave each one a name.

Powers – He saw as a Deer. It's a divining spirit, a Jezebel spirit and a Counterfeit spirit bringing deception.
Principalities – Was shown him as a Cat, representing lasciviousness and lack of moral restraint.
Thrones – Represented by Boar Hog which speaks of uncleanness.
Dominions – Bob saw this as a Giant or Dragon.

But Four Craftsmen are rising in the body of Christ to take authority over these four mystic forces. They are inspired teachers, prophets, apostles, and evangelists who will pull the sword from the Rock to cut away heresy. They will stand on the TRUTH and not back down. They will beat down these for horns and restore families, towns, cities, states, and nations.

*And I said, "What are these coming to do?" So he said, "These are the horns that scattered Judah, so that no one could lift up his head; but the craftsmen are coming to terrify them, to cast out the horns of the nations that lifted up their horn against the land of Judah to scatter it." **(Zechariah 1:21)***

July 3, 2024, marks 40 years since Bob's visitation with Jesus and we've seen many things have transpired since that time. Today we are witnessing the restoration of David's Tabernacle, and the dread champions are on the front lines. We continue to see the rise of the four horns. However, the four craftsmen are endued with Dunamis power because "Excalibur" has been pulled from the Rock of Ages and the power of this fiery sword is risen in the remnant. And they are coming together as an army to do business with the enemy forces of evil on the earth today.

*For behold, the Lord will come with fire, and with his Chariots like a whirlwind to render His anger with fury, and His rebuke with flames of fire. For by fire and His sword the Lord will judge all flesh; and the slain of the Lord shall be many. **(Isaiah 66:15-16)***

Behold in this day, says the Lord, I am bringing forth My fiery sword, bringing forth My Truth and Justice. There will be no doubt when power is released by the Sword of My Spirit, action will be manifest in the earth. Amen.

3

Lift your eyes now and look from the place where you are~

Year of Open Doors of Opportunity

2024 is the Year of Open Door of Opportunity! This is an invitation to enter through three open doors in the Book of Revelation. On Day of Atonement the Lord asked me, "Who is willing and who is ready to step through these doors? Are you? Do you love the Lord with all your heart and serve His Kingdom? Have you placed yourself upon the mercy seat for others not yourself? "These are the questions the Lord asked me, and I answered each one. Yet I asked Him to tell me because only He knows the true intent of my heart. And I believe He is asking His Bride these questions today and each one must answer for themself. This invitation is not only an opportunity to dine with Him, but to boldly enter the throne room of heaven where mysteries are revealed.

The Lord said, "You are going to see many challenges in the coming year but each one carries a greater reward of value as you conquer each one. Know this, the challenge is the enemy's way of trying to prevent you from succeeding in Me. However, you are already equipped with success and must walk past each roadblock and barrier he sets before you. They are not mountains; no, they are mole hills. They are only mountains if you lose perspective of the success that you already are in Me. Conquer each one with love and confidence and continue walking." Amen.

I always appreciate it when the Lord gives me a head's up especially when He forewarns me of the enemy's plan. Sometimes it's vague and other times it's detailed but I know the enemy's objective is to derail what God has planned for good. I realize there will be challenges but we have already been equipped with every good thing we need to succeed in Him. If God is for me who can be against me? (Romans 8:31) I've been given all kingdom authority and walk in its' power and might. (Matthew 28:18-20) I am the head and not the tail, (Deuteronomy 28:13) and no weapon formed against me shall prosper, (Isaiah 54:17) for greater is He who is in me than he who is in this world. (1 John 4:4) The devil is a defeated foe, and he knows it. We cannot take a back seat to him; we must advance forward in power and might!

We're at a Red Sea Moment

I heard the Lord say, "The body of Christ is at a "Red Sea" moment, and it must decide if it will turn and face its enemies, or does it face the supernatural faith of God? He said, I am the Way and the only way to victory. There is no other way!"

Let's take a look at Moses and his Red Sea moment. When his door of opportunity opened, Moses led the children of Israel out of Egypt after God killed all the Egyptians' firstborn. (Exodus 13:15) God led them around by way of the wilderness of the Red Sea. And the LORD went before them by day in a pillar of cloud to lead the way, and by night in a pillar of fire to give them light, so as to go by day and night. He did not take away the pillar of cloud by day or the pillar of fire by night from before the people. (Exodus 13:21-22)

In Exodus 14 God gives Moses a heads up on what's going to take place. God tells him, "I will harden Pharaoh's heart, so that he will pursue them; and I will gain honor over Pharaoh and over all his army, that the Egyptians may know that I am the LORD." And they did so. Of course, by now the Israelites voiced their opinion that they should have remained in bondage in Egypt. Moses had the sure word from God saying they would prevail and be victorious over Pharoah's army. Moses told the people, "Do not be afraid. Stand still, and see the salvation of the LORD, which He will accomplish for you today. For the Egyptians whom you see today, you shall see again no more forever. The LORD will fight for you, and you shall hold your peace." (verse 13-14)

Moses spoke to them with confidence and boldness, yet obviously wavered in his faith. Did he hear God correctly? They're up against the Red Sea with no place to go and the Pharaoh's chariots are in hot pursuit. Although Moses experienced supernatural miracles in Egypt, now he's faced with approximately 2 million discontent Israelites. I don't blame him. I would have been crying out to God too. Moses' lack of faith brought rebuke as well as instruction. And the LORD said to Moses, "Why do you cry to Me? Tell the children of Israel to go forward. But lift your rod and stretch out your hand over the sea and divide it. And the children of Israel shall go on dry ground through the midst of the sea. (verse 15-16)

God's plan was to show Himself strong through them by defeating Pharaoh's army. He would harden the hearts of the Egyptians once again and destroy all of Pharaoh's army, his chariots, and his horsemen. (verse 18) And look what God did next. The Angel of God, who went before the camp of Israel, moved, and went behind them; and the pillar of cloud went from before them and stood behind them. So, it came between the camp of the Egyptians and the camp of Israel. Thus, it was a cloud and darkness to the one, and it gave light by night to the other, so that the one did not come near the other all that night. (verse 19-20) Therefore the Lord reversed position and stood as a fire between the children of Israel and their enemies.

God's arm is not short that He cannot defeat your enemies today. I believe that oftentimes we are unaware of how God works in our life. Many times, He moves obstacles out of the way. Other times He puts obstacles in our way to prevent us from falling into a ditch or going into error. Sometimes He is the cloud by day to deliver us without interference, while other times He is the fire by night to give us clear vision. Yet at other times God sends the fire to protect us and blind the enemy's eyes. Sometimes we think it's just coincidental, where in reality it's divine intervention.

In the eternal realm we already have the victory. And as Christians mature in the Holy Spirit, they become better equipped to follow the cloud or be protected by the fire. I challenge you to think about different times in your own life when circumstances arose that were unexplainable. Truly it was the hand of God moving on your behalf to get you where you needed to be or prevent you from an accident or some form of misfortune. Perhaps your bank account was frozen, and you thought it was the enemy. What you didn't know is that your debit card was confiscated, and someone would have stolen your finances. Certainly, God works in mysterious ways.

Thirty, Sixty or a Hundredfold

Here's a good example of what often takes place in a Christian's life. After hearing the voice of the Lord, they begin their journey of obeying and following new instructions. However, they lose faith and hope when distractions, and challenges begin. They start doubting the voice of God instead of fully trusting Him and stretching forth their rod of authority in the Spirit. If they don't strengthen themselves in the Lord, they'll lose hope and fall into the trap of the enemy instead of walking in victory.

The Lord said, "Doors of opportunity are opening for His bride to enter through. She's being given choices to make and depending on the choice she makes will determine the amount of victory she receives thirty, sixty or a hundredfold. You see not everyone who enters through the door shall receive a hundredfold. The victory comes according to obedience and inheritance."

First, they must hear God's voice and obey, then they can enter through the door of opportunity. There are many doors, and one leads to another. Some people will think this is it. Some will stop and set up camp, but then stop listening. Yet the wise ones indulge in blessings where they camp but continue to listen and obey. They will then have opportunity to move on through the next door and so on.

Abraham didn't stay in one place but followed God when He moved. Abraham moved approximately 17 times in his life's journey. Each one opened another door of opportunity. I believe our inheritance is tied to the land we possess through obedience. In Genesis 12, Terah, left Ur of the Chaldeans taking his son Abraham and grandson Lot with him as well as other family members. Terah died in Haran. Then God spoke to Abraham to leave his father's house and by faith go to a land God would show him. And there he would receive a blessing. So, he departed but took Lot with him. (Genesis 12:1-4) Lot was never part of Abraham's journey and God couldn't fully bless him until they came to a parting of their ways. I believe people oftentimes make the same mistake today. They take too many people and other things with them that become a hindrance. I have always believed that Abraham was only supposed to take his wife Sarah and perhaps "their" household servants and livestock and leave everything else behind.

And the Lord said to Abram, after Lot had separated from him: "Lift your eyes now and look from the place where you are—northward, southward, eastward, and westward; for all the land which you see I give to you and your descendants forever. And I will make your descendants as the dust of the earth; so that if a man could number the dust of the earth, then your descendants also could be numbered. Arise, walk in the land through its length and its width, for I give it to you." Then Abram moved his tent and went and dwelt by the terebinth trees of Mamre, which are in Hebron, and built an altar there to the Lord." **(Genesis 13:14-18)**

Abraham was a blessed man because of his faith and God counted it as righteousness. (Genesis 15:6) God's hand of favor was always on his life; therefore, he dwelled in the blessings of God. However, there were different times when he received a greater portion of blessings, and these were tied to the location where he settled. Thirtyfold after he separated from Lot, sixtyfold with the birth of his son Isaac, and a hundredfold at Mount Moriah. For it was there God told Abraham that in his seed all nations of the earth would be blessed because he obeyed God's voice by not withholding his son, Isaac. (Genesis 22:18) Another hundredfold blessing came after he tithed a tenth of all of his belongings to Melchizedek, the king of Salem. (Genesis 14:18-20) After that, God gave him the promise of the land his descendants would inherit. (Genesis 15:1-21)

There are also times we receive thirtyfold blessings and at other times sixty or a hundredfold. I believe that all born again Christians live in the blessings of God. We are the seed of Abraham the father of faith and therefore entitled to receive spiritual blessings. Many of them are tied to the land we possess. No matter where our physical location is we remain blessed. However, being in the right location increases our ability to receive more abundantly. We may receive thirtyfold in one location yet in another a hundredfold where it seems like the blessings are chasing us down. Although we may relocate and become complacent. By our own hand we limit our blessing and therefore only receive thirtyfold. That's why it's important we continue to hear and obey and not let our guard down. We must be willing to leave Haran for Beersheba.

Please don't misunderstand, I'm not saying we need to pack things up and move to another town or state. Perhaps that will be necessary for some people, however, this could relate to many things. It could be a job relocation across town or in the same building. You may be blessed a hundredfold in your current job but get transferred to a different department and everything goes sour. What looks like a promotion – isn't. The blessing was tied to the old position.

God is not short in blessing His children. However, they are short in hearing and shorter yet in obeying. Some become complacent, comfy in their camp. Many have followed man's voice and it caused them to be in the wrong place for seasons in their life. But God is speaking loud and clear to those who have an ear to hear. Let there be no mistake, He's uprooting many and bringing them into the land of plenty. Some have been in dry and arid places but that's about to change. And what was dry for one will be an oasis for another.

Doors Of Opportunity

Let's look at some doors of opportunity in scripture. Right now, we're in the middle of the greatest harvest of souls the world has ever experienced. However, many Christians are still shying away from their responsibility to witness to the lost. Every born-again Christian has been given the Great Commission; this is the commandment from the Lord before He ascended. The entire body of Christ is commissioned to carry on where He left off. He gave all authority to the body of believers so why do many make excuses, roll up the carpet or throw in the towel?

The Great Commission is given in both Matthew and Mark. However, Mark 16:17-18) adds the signs that follow the believer who live according to the Great Commission.

*And Jesus came and spoke to them, saying, "All authority has been given to Me in heaven and on earth. Go therefore and make disciples of all the nations, baptizing them in the name of the Father and of the Son and of the Holy Spirit, teaching them to observe all things that I have commanded you; and lo, I am with you always, even to the end of the age." **(Matthew 28:18-20)***

*And He said to them, "Go into all the world and preach the gospel to every creature. He who believes and is baptized will be saved; but he who does not believe will be condemned. And these signs will follow those who believe: In My name they will cast out demons; they will speak with new tongues; they will take up serpents; and if they drink anything deadly, it will by no means hurt them; they will lay hands on the sick, and they will recover." **(Mark 16:15-18)***

More people have a born-again experience outside the four walls of the church. Many have a one-on-one encounter with a stranger who took time to witness to them. Many people are good excuse makers. You don't have to be an ordained minister or evangelist to spread the Good News! If you're born again then Christ, the anointed One lives inside you and draws near to the lost. So why do Christians keep Him for themselves? They make excuses like; I'm too shy, I'm too busy, I'm in a hurry, I won't know what to say. Or maybe they don't want to hear about Jesus, I think they already know Him. What if they won't accept Him or what if they won't accept me? I just feel awkward. However freely we received salvation and freely we're to share this precious gift of eternal life. The door of opportunity that's always open is salvation and Its name is Jesus Christ. In this time of great harvest, this door is open wide for all who are willing to enter in.

Remember this, you might be the only "Jesus" someone will encounter, and it might be the most unlikely time or place. But God puts people in our path so we can be a light in a dark place and witness to lost souls. Our greatest witness is how we live our daily life. People pay attention to how we act, interact, and respond in everyday situations.

Peter's Open Door

Peter, a devout Jew had an experience that changed his way of thinking and his entire life. One day he became very hungry and fell into a trance, he saw heaven opening and an object like a great sheet bound at the four corners, descending to the earth. In it were all kinds of four-footed animals of the earth, wild beasts, creeping things, and birds of the air. And a voice came to him, "Rise, Peter; kill and eat." But Peter said, "Not so, Lord! For I have never eaten anything common or unclean." And a voice spoke to him again the second time, "What God has cleansed you must not call common." This was done three times. And the object was taken up into heaven again. (Acts 10:10-14)

Shortly thereafter Peter was summoned to Cornelius' home. Cornelius was a Roman centurion who feared God and gave alms to the needy. When Peter arrived, he told him about his encounter with the Lord. Cornelius knew Peter would come to his home and he welcomed the word of the Lord. Peter's opportunity took root when he opened his mouth and said: "In truth I perceive that God shows no partiality. But in every nation whoever fears Him and works righteousness is accepted by Him." (verse 34-35) Peter preached the gospel to Cornelius' whole household. And while Peter was still speaking these words, the Holy Spirit fell upon all those who heard the word. And those of the circumcision who believed were astonished, as many as came with Peter, because the gift of the Holy Spirit had been poured out on the Gentiles also. For they heard them speak with tongues and magnify God. (verse 44)

Talk about an open door of opportunity! Peter opened the door for salvation to come to the Gentiles. Up to this point it was only for the Jew. But it was Peter's choice to accept or reject the vision of unclean animals as well as the invitation to Cornelius' home. God has far greater plans for each one of us if we are willing to hear and obey. Each door that opens is opportunity for advancement in the kingdom of God and more and more doors will open on purpose.

Paul's Open Doors

The apostle Paul mentions several times that doors of opportunity were open to him. In first Corinthians 16, he planned to go through the region of Macedonia, visiting Corinth. But things happened differently than he planned. Instead, Paul made a soon painful visit to Corinth to personally confront them in some areas. He said he would tarry in Ephesus for a "great and effectual" door was open to him. Paul knew that God had given him opportunity now in Ephesus. Paul wisely relied on his own desires, but also on God's open doors. Paul knew that opposition often accompanies opportunities.

I will remain in Ephesus [however] until Pentecost, for a wide door of opportunity for effectual [service] has opened to me [there, a great and promising one], and [there are] many adversaries. **(1 Corinthians 16:8-9 AMPC)**

Acts 19 speaks both of opportunities and opposition Paul had while in Ephesus at this time. Paul found some disciples and asked if they received the Holy Spirit when they believed? They never heard about the Holy Spirit; they were only baptized into John's baptism. Then Paul said, "John indeed baptized with a baptism of repentance, saying to the people that they should believe on Him who would come after him, that is, on Christ Jesus." When they heard this, they were baptized in the name of the Lord Jesus. And when Paul had laid hands on them, the Holy Spirit came upon them, and they spoke with tongues and prophesied. (verse 2-6) And God worked unusual miracles by the hands of Paul, so that even handkerchiefs or aprons were brought from his body to the sick, and the diseases left them, and the evil spirits went out of them. (verse 11-12) He was also confronted by exorcists and magicians, but the word of the Lord grew mightily and prevailed. (verse 20)

I want to point out something in the preceding paragraph. Over the years the Lord has emphasized the importance of baptism immediately following conversion, then the infilling of the Holy Spirit. Why? It's like the Parable of the Sower in Matthew chapter 13. All the seed comes from the same bag however it falls on 4 different types of soil and of course 3 of the 4 are lost. Only the one sowed on good soil yielded crop, some a hundredfold, some sixty, some thirty. The Lord told me that Holy Spirit is like the good soil because once He dwells within the believer, He will convict them of their sin nature. Then when temptation comes crouching at their door they will not fall into the trap of the enemy. (Genesis 4:7) Until the soil is cultivated by Holy Spirit hearts remain stony and fall prey to the enemy when he comes to choke out the seeds of righteousness through deceit, unbelief, and the religious spirit.

If you do well, will you not be accepted? And if you do not do well, sin crouches at your door; its desire is for you, but you must master it. **(Genesis 4:7 AMPC)**

Open Doors in Revelation

The last open door in Scripture is Revelations 4:1, it's the one at the beginning of this chapter. Bob Jones always said that the Book of Revelation is a love letter to His Bride. Although the next two open doors were written to the Churches of Philadelphia and Laodicea, I believe they represent the refining process the remnant goes through to receive an invitation to the "open door" of Revelation 4:1.

Philadelphia - These things says He who is holy, He who is true, "He who has the key of David, He who opens and no one shuts, and shuts and no one opens." "I know your works. See, I have set before you an open door, and no one can shut it; for you have a little strength, have kept My word, and have not denied My name. **(Revelation 3:7-8)**

To the remnant of Philadelphia, He who is holy and true, holds the "Key of David" (Isaiah 22:22) and Christ alone has authority to open this door. He alone prevents anyone else from closing it. There are three conditions in Revelation 3:9 that qualify them. First, they have little strength which means they live by faith. James 2:24 says that a man is justified by works, and not by faith only. Yet the remnant's faith works through love. (Galatians 5:6) Second, they have kept His Word; therefore, they did not compromise the Gospel. And third, they have not denied His name, His name is Love. (1John 4:8) Therefore, Love holds the "Key of David" to unlock this door so the faithful remnant who abides in Love (John 15:20) may proceed.

Laodicea - As many as I love, I rebuke and chasten. Therefore, be zealous and repent. Behold, I stand at the door and knock. If anyone hears My voice and opens the door, I will come in to him and dine with him, and he with Me. To him who overcomes I will grant to sit with Me on My throne, as I also overcame and sat down with My Father on His throne. (Revelation 3:19-21)

Only Christ could open the first door, and it was the remnants' faith working through Love that put them in position to gain more access. However, the Laodicean remnant contains overcomers because they overcome the lukewarm spirit. When He chastised them for their lukewarm Christianity, they quickly repented. Now they're granted permission to open the door because the Lord is standing on the other side and knocking. But the key is this, they must be attentive to hear His voice and open it. And because they did, they're invited to come in and dine with Him and granted permission to sit down with Papa on His throne.

Throne Room of Heaven

After these things I looked, and behold, a door standing open in heaven. And the first voice which I heard was like a trumpet speaking with me, saying, "Come up here, and I will show you things which must take place after this." **(Revelation 4:1)**

Jesus opened the door to the faithful remnant. It was their faith working through Love that gave them access. After the Laodicean remnant repented and overcame their lukewarmness He knocked on their door with a dinner invitation in His hand. There's a progression taking place here. Because the remnant's faith that works through Love, Jesus opens the door of opportunity. And it is here a greater level of faith is required. After the Lord's rebuke the remnant must do a thorough self-examination. He said, "You are neither cold nor hot. But because you are lukewarm, I will vomit you out of My mouth. Because you say, I am rich, have become wealthy, and have need of nothing and do not know that you are wretched, miserable, poor, blind, and naked." (Revelation 3:15-17) But He said, "I know your works!" Their works by faith got them thus far but there's a lot of baggage attached. Because He loves them, He corrects them. He said, "As many as I love, I rebuke and chasten. Therefore, be zealous and repent." (Revelation 3:19) Their love for Him caused them to repent quickly which qualified them for entrance to this door.

This is the bride's invitation to enter the throne room of heaven. The door is standing open and there is no need to knock. There is nothing to prevent the remnant from entering through this door. This is where the Bride of Christ rests in Holy Spirit and receives pertinent revelation. Here is where wisdom and understanding reside and spiritual knowledge is imparted. Mysteries of Scripture are understood and released to the remnant's spirit. As I spoke earlier in chapter 1 about the eternal realm, the throne room is open and available for the remnant who has an ear to hear what the Spirit is saying to the churches of Revelation. And all who enter shall join the angels who worship day and night saying, "Holy, holy, holy, Lord God Almighty, Who was and is and is to come!" (verse 8b)

4

There's a great spirit of offense that lingers in the body of Christ and we are not entitled to this.

Year of the Woman

Kathryn Kuhlman Prophecy

2024 or 5784 on the Hebrew calendar is the "Year of the Open Door." It's the "Door of Opportunity" and it's standing open in heaven with an invitation for His Bride to "Come up here" (Revelation 4:1) so He can show her things that will shortly take place. He's preparing and making ready His Bride for the end of the age. There are things hidden from mankind, things the body of believers were not privileged to have knowledge of until this time. (Isaiah 48:6-7)

You have heard; see all this. And will you not declare it? I have made you hear new things from this time, even hidden things, and you did not know them. They are created now and not from the beginning; and before this day you have not heard them, lest you should say, 'Of course I knew them.' ***(Isaiah 48:6-7)***

First, I want to share the dream and then take it apart to discover some interesting facts that I believe are pertinent to the current day.

Katherine Kuhlman Dream

From June 1, 2014

On June 1st this year I had what I believe was a dream within a dream. For the most part, I was only an observer, yet it was so vivid and real that I felt it significant to share with the body of believers. The time of harvest is quickly approaching, and we must be ready.

In this dream the date was October 16, 2014. I observed Kathryn Kuhlman standing on stage wearing her long flowing white dress with her left arm outstretched. Her boney index finger was pointing at the audience as she began to prophecy.

"All those born on October 16th have a special anointing. And there's a special anointing being released to the body and it's very powerful!"

The scene quickly changed, and I was standing outside where I observed ancient black wrought iron gates. They were rather scary looking because of their size and age. These ancient gates were perhaps twelve feet high and thirty feet in length. They were attached to a black stone wall on either side like a fortress. The gates had been closed and locked for many, many years. As I looked closer, I could see thousands of people standing behind the closed gates. In fact, I could see no end to this massive gathering of people. There were people from every tongue, tribe, and nation. But in unity, as one body, they all worked together to push open the gates. Then breaking through the darkness into the light, they all ran quickly to receive this anointing Kathryn Kuhlman prophesied and released.

(End of dream.)

Understanding Today

In this dream there were ancient gates that had been closed for a very long time, however through a spirit of unity people pushed the gates open. October 16, 2024, will be 10 years since this prophetic dream took place. Prophetically the number 10 represents several things including law, order, government, and restoration. I believe this year we will begin to see civil law and order restored in our nation. The Apostolic government in the body of Christ will arise to a new standard of honor, hope, truth, and love. The mechanical bull is being replaced by the headship of Jesus Christ. And this year marks the beginning of the restoration of all things according to Acts 3:18-21.

But those things which God foretold by the mouth of all His prophets, that the Christ would suffer, He has thus fulfilled. Repent therefore and be converted, that your sins may be blotted out, so that times of refreshing may come from the presence of the Lord, and that He may send Jesus Christ, who was preached to you before, whom heaven must receive until the times of restoration of all things, which God has spoken by the mouth of all His holy prophets since the world began. **(Acts 3:18-21)**

Here's what I find significant. The date of the dream was June 1, however in the dream it was October 16. Therefore, the dream took place four months into the future. I believe John 4 helps interpret the dream. The Samaritan woman just encountered the Lord and knows that He's the Messiah. She ran back to her village to spread the Good News. She's the first person in scripture Christ reveals Himself to and becomes the first evangelist. She tells everyone in Sychar about her encounter with Messiah at the well. And she's been given a new lease on life through the living water. The whole town witnesses her transformation and desires to drink of this water also. She runs back to the well and the entire town follows.

In the meantime, the disciples return bringing food and are shocked to see Jesus has interacted with a Samaritan woman at the well. He's not interested in their morsels of food; He's been doing the Father's business. He said to them, "My food is to do the will of Him who sent Me, and to finish His work. (verse 34) Then He said something strange, "Do you not say, there are still four months and then comes the harvest?" Behold, I say to you, lift up your eyes and look at the fields, for they are already white for harvest! (verse 35) When the disciples turned around, they saw everyone from Sychar running toward them. They wanted to meet the Messiah too!

From June to October is four months. Is our harvest not here? Are we overlooking the point? The harvest is upon us but are we doing our part? Jesus said, "He who reaps receives wages, and gathers fruit for eternal life, that both he who sows, and he who reaps may rejoice together. For in this the saying is true: one sows, and another reaps. I sent you to reap that for which you have not labored; others have labored, and you have entered into their labors." (verse 36-38)

All Christians have opportunity to sow seeds unto salvation like the Samaritan woman. However, it's fair to say that not every seed you sow will take root. Yet you may come along later to water a seed someone else sowed. Or perhaps reap the harvest when a seed receives salvation. Perhaps you didn't labor for it, yet you enter the reward of the one who sows and the one who waters. It all pays the same.

Ancient Gates

Let's look at the ancient gates. There were thousands of people on the other side of these gates. And when they came into agreement by a spirit of unity, they pushed open the gates that had been closed for a very long time. I believe these gates needed to remain closed until the time of harvest when the laborers are plentiful. This is the year of the

"Open Doors of Opportunity" and one door that will open widely is power evangelism. Every Christian has a testimony, and each one is given opportunity to share the Good News of Jesus Christ. I believe the body of Christ has been calling unto the Lord of the Harvest to bring in the lost souls.

*Then He said to His disciples, "The harvest truly is plentiful, but the laborers are few. Therefore, pray the Lord of the harvest to send out laborers into His harvest." **(Matthew 9:37-38)***

There remain many ancient gods in existence today throughout the world and many nations still worship them. However, Christian's worship and serve the only living God and now is the time to reap a harvest of souls, including those who worship ancient deities.

In Psalms 24, David is bringing the ark of the covenant back into Jerusalem from the home of Obed-Edom. (2 Samuel 6) When the ark that represented God's presence was captured by the Philistines, Eli's daughter-in-law bore a son and called him Ichabod, saying the glory has departed from Israel because the ark of the covenant was captured. (1 Samuel 4:21) But now when the ark is returning to Jerusalem, the King of glory of heaven and earth was returning. And David was crying out for these ancient gates to be opened so the King of glory could enter.

*Lift up your heads, O you gates; and be lifted up, you age-abiding doors, that the King of glory may come in. Who is the King of glory? The Lord strong and mighty, the Lord mighty in battle. Lift up your heads, O you gates; yes, lift them up, you age-abiding doors, that the King of glory may come in. **(Psalm 24:7-9)***

I believe the ancient gates from this dream represent the gates from Psalm 24. Thousands of people coming through these gates will usher in the presence of God in a spirit of unity, holiness, and love. These doors will swing wide open to let the King of glory pass through. A flood of evangelism will usher in the King of glory. These evangelists will possess Kingdom fire, power, healing, miracles and complete salvation, and so much more!

Women of Mars Hill

In this experience I'm standing in a beautiful green lofty meadow looking into the distance beyond my view. It's early in the morning as the sun begins to rise over the hilltop. In a distance a foggy mist rises up and moves across the summit. As the mist begins to dissipate, I witness the secret that's been hidden within this hill. One by one faces begin to form on its front side in what looks like a bubble or circle. I try to peer closer in the spirit to gain a better visual. As my vision becomes clearer, I see a woman's face inside each circle. No two are the same, yet each circle is equal in size. None of them are known or have a point of influence in society. However, the women are from every nation, tongue, and tribe. As the vision fades away, the hillside is covered with faces of emerging women.

Immediately when I awoke, I knew it was Mars Hill, yet it seemed rather strange. However, is this "not" the year of the woman? Are they "not" the army of God forming to bring the Good News? Psalm 68:11 declares that women bear and publish [the news] are a great host. They bring forth the word of God in power. Is this "not" the secret weapon hidden in the cleft of the Rock waiting to be revealed for such a time as this?

The Lord gives the word [of power]; the women who bear and publish [the news] are a great host. **(Psalm 68:11 AMPC)**

I believe the foggy mist rising over the hilltop is Holy Spirit who's lifting the veil to reveal the bride. She's been hidden in the secret place of the Most High where she abides under the shadow of the Almighty. (Psalm 91:1a) But now He's bringing her out of hiddenness, and she's coming forth in power and might demonstrating Kingdom authority.

Each woman represented in this revelation had equal influence, no one was greater than another. Every circle touched other circles, like a chain link fence. Chain link is woven together to form a diamond like pattern. This pattern is called weaving. Therefore, the end of every diamond shaped link overlaps another and is twisted together which creates its strength. Chain link has an open weave and therefore does not obscure sunlight from either side of the fence. Therefore, I believe this army will be in fellowship with one another. There's a spirit of unity being birthed in the sisterhood to release and bring forth a powerful army in the last days. They will be joined together by Holy Spirit and there shall be no obstruction to God's light. This army of women shall be transparent in nature but strong in the power of His might. (Ephesians 6:10)

Mars Hill

Mars Hill is the Roman name for a hill in Athens, Greece called the hill of Ares or the Areopagus. Rising some 377 feet above the land below and not far from the Acropolis and Agora (marketplace). Mars Hill served as a meeting place for the Areopagus court, the highest court in Greece for civil, criminal, and religious matters. Even under Roman rule in the time of the New Testament, Mars Hill remained an important meeting place where philosophy, religion and law were discussed. **(Per Wikipedia)**

Let's look at what Scripture says about Mars Hill in Acts 17. When Paul arrived in Athens, his spirit was provoked when he saw the city was given over to idols. (verse 16) Immediately he began presenting the gospel to both Jews and Gentiles in the synagogue and marketplace daily – to anyone and everyone – about the resurrection of Christ. Statues of pagan gods were plentiful throughout Athens, and this deeply disturbed him. However, when Paul saw an idol dedicated "TO THE UNKNOWN GOD" he began to open their mind to understanding who this God is. (verse 23-26)

While at the marketplace he encountered some Epicurean and Stoic philosophers (verse 18) who, having heard Paul proclaim the resurrected Jesus Christ, wanted to learn about "this new doctrine" he was teaching. They brought him to the Areopagus to hear more from him. (verse 19-20) Paul observed that they were "very religious", because of the many altars and "objects of worship." (verse 23) But when he saw the altar to the "Unknown God" it was his great opportunity to introduce them to the one true God and the only way of salvation, Jesus Christ.

Are not "all" born again believers called to spread the Good News of Christ resurrection and call sinners to repentance? I believe this is the season women are coming to the forefront to preach and prophesy. They are bold and fearless like Paul on Mars Hill and Peter on the Day of Pentecost. This is the Bride of Christ coming forth in power and might to usher in the kingdom of His light. They are the company of the Good News.

There are many lessons that can be learned from Mars Hill. Although Paul was provoked in his spirit, he presented the gospel to everyone who had an ear to hear. He didn't allow personal feelings to interfere and prevent the opportunity at hand. He presented Christ and the Resurrection. Many were converted, others mocked him while some rejected his message altogether. Yet others were open-minded and desired to hear more. The door of opportunity to salvation was open wide. The ground was fertile, the seed of salvation was planted as Paul boldly proclaimed the Good News.

I believe we're going to see an army of women arise out of the cleft of the Rock and come forward with a powerful anointing. They will preach, prophecy and evangelize by the Spirit of God. They'll demonstrate the "Great Commission" (Matthew 28:19-20) on a consistent basis. I believe new ministries are being formed in this day. The church is often referred to as "she or her". Therefore, I believe the faces on the hill represent ministries that have been preserved for this hour in church history.

Now the anointing is on women in a greater dimension than ever before. In the past we have seen great moves of God through different women. Maria Woodworth-Etter, Aimee Semple McPherson, Kathryn Kuhlman, and Ruth Ward Heflin to name a few. The Holy Spirit moved mightily through each of these women with the manifestation of supernatural faith, healing, and evangelism. Ruth Ward Heflin also had a manifestation of gold dust and miracles. Each of these ministries seem to overlap one another. Miss Heflin died in 2000; since that time there appears to be a vacancy in this type of ministry. I believe we have seen a glimpse of the supernatural manifestations however not on a consistent basis. There has been a vacancy that will now be filled and not just by one woman or a few. It will be a company of women working together in unity led by the Holy Spirit of God.

The Lord has sheltered the women on Mars Hill while training them by His Spirit in humility, love, grace, mercy, and long-suffering. Mankind will see women in the natural but hear the Spirit of God speaking through them. This mighty company of women live in reverential fear and awe of the powerful God they serve.

This is a company of women who bear and publish the Good News. They are a great host who will not back down from the enemy and will not compromise or fall prey to the works of the flesh. They will stand together in unity, like the chain link fence arm in arm. And the "Son" shall shine forth through them releasing power and glory. Get ready for massive waves of salvation, healing and deliverance as this army marches forth to victory in Jesus' name.

Get Over Your Offense

Very clearly, I was shown that 2024 is the year of the woman. And she's coming forth in holy array. However, she must be careful and always on guard for the enemy does not take vacations. He's lurking at every corner for opportunities to keep her from following the Lord and launch out into the deep. He has several strategies to achieve his goal. First comes distraction and unbelief. If he can distract her from hearing God, she'll follow the dictates of her heart instead of His divine will. Then she'll fall into unbelief because confusion set in. Once she begins down this rabbit trail it becomes easier to be thrown off course. Doubt sets in and she wonders if she's even going in the right direction and then flounders. Temptation lurks at the door, and she feels so far from God because weariness is setting in.

One clever scheme of the devil is to wear out the saints. (Daniel 7:25 AMPC). His main goal is to get her offended. Once offended, she no longer sees or hears clearly from Holy Spirit. Everything is filtered through a spirit of offense because she lacks discernment. Since she no longer rests in the mind of Christ, she operates from her soul not her spirit. And now her words have a bitter and critical edge instead of kindness, mercy, grace, and love. With a critical spirit she joins forces with the enemy through the very words she speaks. By this time, she's far enough off course but can't realize it. She's still floundering and trying to find her way. Remember, the enemy only has power through the spoken words of the saints. If he can keep her offended, he usurps her authority in that area. Then she becomes the victim not the victor because she has played into the craftiness of his hand.

But do not be discouraged, Romans 8:37 says that we are more than conquerors and gain a surpassing victory through Christ who loved us. Before the foundation of the world God knew that we would have these challenges, but He equipped us with every good thing to overcome the enemy's strategies. Think about it, the battle has already been won, the cross of suffering is our victory. We must always remain prayerful and reassured of God's promises in the written word. Paul says to pray in the Spirit because the Spirit knows what we need.

Likewise, the Spirit also helps in our weaknesses. For we do not know what we should pray for as we ought, but the Spirit Himself makes intercession for us with groanings which cannot be uttered. **(Romans 8:26)**

When temptation comes knocking at the door of our mind, we must rule over it. (Genesis 4:6-7) If not, we start doubting what God said and become like Eve in the garden. When the serpent spoke to her he posed a question, "Did God indeed say?" (Genesis 3:1) And this prompted her to doubt. She already knew what God said but he planted a seed of doubt in her mind. Then she agreed with it and acted accordingly upon it. In the same way today, the enemy wastes no time coming to steal God's plan from His children. When we know God has spoken and given a course of direction to follow, we must rule over the deceiving spirit of the enemy.

So, the LORD *said to Cain, "Why are you angry? And why has your countenance fallen? If you do well, will you not be accepted? And if you do not do well, sin lies at the door. And its desire is for you, but you should rule over it."* ***(Genesis 4:6-7)***

We must embrace the wisdom of God and His righteousness and know that His word never fails. We must rule over our thoughts by embracing His. We've been given the most powerful weapon on earth, the power of the word of God. And when we speak, it becomes a sharp two-edged sword. The body of Christ needs to believe what the word of God says and release the promises. There's power in our words. Too often Christians want to give their power to the enemy. And this is his goal, to use the power of God's children for his purpose. When we embrace doubt, unbelief, and temptation, we fall directly into the enemy's trap. Then we begin spewing untruths from our mouth and the enemy uses it for his benefit. A baby Christian has little power. But a seasoned Christian gains power and authority during their spiritual journey. When they become offended and speak from a place of offense, it does great damage to everyone concerned. Indeed, we have then lorded our authority over to the enemy and he uses it against us. This must stop!

Dream About Offense

In this dream I was up for a great promotion by the Lord. I was given a little red sports car convertible, and its top was down. This speaks of the power of the blood of Jesus, (red) acceleration, (sports car) and open heaven revelation (convertible). Convertible also speaks of converts – evangelism. The increase, the promotion was right at my door. The little red sports car pulled up to the curb in front of my house. There was no doubt, it was mine! As I walked toward it, a female church leader picked me up in her arms and ran with me. Then she stopped and tossed me over a redwood fence. I was surprised! I was not hurt however I was certainly startled. She looked at me and sternly said, "You need to get over your offense!" Immediately I sought the Lord about my offense. Why was I offended? Who was I offended with? If you ask the Lord, He is faithful to reveal the secrets of your heart so you can repent. He desires us to be free of all sin including offense. Holding on to my offense keeps me in bondage to it and gives the enemy authority over me in that area.

The woman in this dream represents the church. There's been too much offense inside the four walls of the church. Church leaders are offended amongst themselves. The laity is offended amongst themselves. Worship teams are offended with one another. There's just a great spirit of offense that lingers in the body of Christ and we are not entitled to this. Christ took our offence on the cross. So why do we continuously pick it up, nurse it, babysit it and nurture it? It's like we want it to graduate with a master's degree. We want to hold on to it and feel we have a right to keep it.

It's time to get over our offense, give it to God and leave it there. Don't pick it up again. Turn your back on it and walk away. Leave it at the foot of the cross of Christ.

Immediately following my repentance, I walked over and got in the passenger seat of the sports car; Holy Spirit is my driver. Lots of people began to surround my new car and suddenly the Father pointed His finger in my face and said, "It's the year of the woman!" Once I repented of my offense, I was forgiven then immediately launched into power evangelism. There was no delay! (End of dream.) But let me mention that previously I saw the Father distributing "The Bread of Life." Now it's time that women go forth in power spreading the Good News!

The Lord gives the word [of power]; the women who bear and publish [the news] are a great host. **(Psalm 68:11)**

I have no doubt that 2024 is the year women are coming to the forefront of ministry. This dream is an indication of what God is doing through women in ministry today. It is time in church history for women to arise to their call. I'm not putting a greater emphasis on women; it is the anointing that is launching them forward. The body is not complete without woman. We will discuss that in the next chapter. Mankind will recognize the Spirit of God speaking through the vessel known as woman and will not be able to deny it. Oh yes, I believe man will still try to shut women down, because the church has been male dominated for so long. But God will make a way for His voice to be heard. Women need to keep their slate clean through repentance and not allow the enemy access through offense.

No Christian can allow offense in their life. We must allow the Wisdom of the Ages, Holy Spirit who lives within us, to guide and direct us. We need to check ourselves daily, and sometimes hourly to know if we are in a offense or not. Recently I've been given many opportunities to get offended. I could feel the offense trying to rise and at that point I made a choice to receive or reject the offense. Choosing wisely, I gave the offense to the Lord. Scripture says that He is to carry our burden (Psalm 55:22) and I am to be His vessel in the earth today doing the work He gave me to do without hindrance from the enemy. We overcome by the blood of the Lamb and the word of our testimony, (Revelation 12:11) which is the Lord Jesus Christ our Savior.

Cast your burden on the Lord [releasing the weight of it] and He will sustain you; He will never allow the [consistently] righteous to be moved (made to slip, fall, or fail). Remember this, we cannot carry offense into this outpouring of the Holy Spirit. Offense will disqualify you; grace will promote you. **(Psalm 55:22 AMPC)**

5

You can enter when you are ready.

No Trespassing

He Who Has An Ear Let Him Hear

During the Day of Atonement this year I had opportunity to be in Ohio with my family. I have two great nieces that would be married two weeks apart from each other. I decided to drive instead of fly and stay instead of making two round trips. One of my family members was leaving on vacation and invited me to stay at their house while they were gone. It was incredibly quiet and peaceful plus a great time to hear from the Lord. Something I also found quite interesting, both of my younger brother's birthdays fell in this time frame. So, I had the opportunity to share their special days with them. I believe this was part of God's plan because He gave me opportunity to sow into both their lives - in person. It's so exciting to see how God is working His divine will into the lives of my close family members. God is so good and always faithful.

The "No Trespassing" revelation is not mine; it belongs to my brother Rick. With his permission I'm going to share it later in this chapter. I told my brother to pay attention to his dreams when he went to bed on the eve of Atonement. That night he had an incredible visitation and it's not only worthy but necessary to share in this book. Although it was personal to him, it's pertinent for the whole body of Christ. Remember God speaks to all His children, not just a few. He speaks to everyone who has an ear to hear.

In the parable of the sower of the seed (Mark 4) Jesus first describes the four types of soil that the seed falls upon. Remember, it's all the same seed, it comes from the same bag. It's the ground that we must be concerned with here. Some seed fell by the wayside and the birds came and devoured it. Some fell on stony ground, but it had no depth of earth, and the sun scorched it. Because it had no root it withered away. Some fell among the thorns, and they choked it out and it yielded no crop. But other seed fell on good ground and yielded crops, some thirty-fold, some sixty-fold, and some hundred-fold. Then Jesus said, "He who has ears to hear, let him hear!"

And He said to them, "He who has ears to hear, let him hear!" (Mark 4:9 & 23)

God is speaking to His children today. He is sowing seed to all those who have an ear to hear. Oftentimes we become too busy and choose not to hear what the Lord is saying. We must not become like the children of Israel. God gave them a promise that all would be well with them if they would obey His voice. However, they chose not to hear it. You see when you hear His voice, then you must obey what He says. And often that can be tough. Everyone wants to hear God's voice, but obeying is another thing. Obedience requires discipline and often sacrifice as well. It means "no compromise." Not everything the Lord ask of you is easy. Many times, it's a difficult task or perhaps a difficult word you need to present to an individual or perhaps the body of Christ. The children of Israel took the easy way out. They sent Moses to hear God's voice. And Moses reaped the hundred-fold reward whereas that whole generation died in the wilderness. Moses saw God face to face and His glory rested upon him. Oh yes, Moses had a difficult task, in fact I would say it was impossible. Yet with God nothing is impossible. (Luke 1:37)

*But this is what I commanded them, saying, Obey My voice, and I will be your God, and you shall be My people. And walk in all the ways that I have commanded you, that it may be well with you. Yet they did not obey or incline their ear but followed the counsels and the dictates of their evil hearts and went backward and not forward. **(Jeremiah 7:23-24)***

Notice that in the parable of the Sower, Jesus makes this statement twice. And He said to them, "He who has ears to hear, let him hear!" (Mark 4:9 & 23) The first time is after He describes the four types of soil that the seed falls upon. (verse 9) The second time is after He explains that nothing is hidden that will not be revealed, nor has anything been kept secret but that it should not come to light. Then He again repeats the statement, "He who has an ear to ear let him hear!" (verse 23) You see God cannot reveal certain secrets until a fullness of time in our life. Why? We aren't mature enough to handle it. Just like you can't give a newborn baby a bicycle nor can you give a three-year old the keys to your Mercedes.

When we're maturing in our spiritual walk, God reveals what He needs us to know that brings us to a certain point of faith and greater hunger for Holy Spirit. The more we hunger and thirst for spiritual growth, the greater our faith and trust grow in Him. And each act of obedience helps thrust us forward to the promises He holds for our lives. One time the Lord told me that if He revealed everything He had for me all at once, I would explode! I wouldn't be able to handle it. That's why He only gives us a little at a time. It's like climbing a ten-foot ladder, you must take each wrung at a time.

Believers have a promise that if they seek first the kingdom of God and His righteousness, all these things shall be added to them. (Matthew 6:33) So what are these things? All the promises of yes and amen God purposed for us individually before the foundation of the earth. He gave us everything we need to fulfill His purpose for our existence on this earth for His kingdom. That's why it's vital that we hear and obey His voice. Mark 4:24 says to take heed what we hear. With the same measure you use, it will be measured to you; and to you who hear, more will be given. When we climb that ten-foot ladder one rung at a time, He adds increase. Verse 25a says that whoever has, to him more will be given.

Therefore, He continues to grant us greater revelation and understanding because we continue seeking His kingdom. But we're given a warning in 25b, He says, "But whoever does not have, even what he has will be taken away from him." If we become dull in spirit and decide not to hear His voice and/or obey, our favor wanes. If we no longer want to hear Him, we literally shut the door to His blessings and chose not to receive them. He won't force feed us. However, He will woo us back to Him, if we have an ear to hear. Romans 11:29 says, For the gifts and calling of God are without repentance. "Without repentance" means that God won't change His mind about what He has called you to do. If God has called you, that calling is still there, whether or not you have obeyed. However, you cannot reap a hundred-fold harvest if you stop mid-stream or halfway up the ladder.

The Revelation

With great enthusiasm Rick called me early the next morning to share his experience from the night before. His experience began like a dream. Rick said he was walking down a path when he saw a brown wooden fence ahead of him. As he approached it, he saw a wooden sign hanging from it. The sign was brown, and the words "No Trespassing" were written with black paint. As he drew closer, he saw a man approaching from the other side of the fence. Rick could see the man was very handsome, more handsome than any man he'd ever seen. He was wearing a white shirt and brown trousers. His eyes were like deep blue pools and his hair was brown.

Now they were standing across from each other only separated by the fence. Rick asked the man what is on the other side? The man said, "You know what's beyond!" Rick responded that all he saw was trees, grass, and fields and it was all quite beautiful. The man told him, you should know! Rick said, well I don't know but I'd like to find out! The man said, "Are you ready?" Rick thought for a second and said, "I think so." The man said, "You can enter when you are ready." That's when Rick woke up.

The Offense

A few hours later while Rick was meditating, he heard a still small voice say, "I overlook your dirty jokes and smoking for now, but I won't overlook it forever!" At that point Rick knew – the beautiful man he saw earlier at the fence was the Lord. And it's like the handwriting is on the wall. It's time for decision making.

Rick has 2 vices. Cigarettes and joke telling. He's been a heavy cigarette smoker since he was a teenager. And because he loves to hear people laugh, he enjoys telling jokes. However, some of his jokes were sexually motivated. Months ago, I told him he needs to decide which side of the fence he's on. He tells me jokes too. Funny jokes, some that don't make any sense but they're cute. He used to tell me dirty jokes until I told him about the fence. In recent months he quit telling me dirty jokes, he saved them for the mailman or other victims. Proverbs 17:22 says a merry heart is like a good medicine and I agree with being joyful. I believe that when the Lord showed him the error of his way, he was given a choice to make. And I praise God He faithfully continues to show me the error of my ways to keep me on the straight and narrow.

When I think of the word fence, I think of offense. In chapter 4, I was tossed over the fence before I could enter the future destiny for my life. I believe that's what the Lord is saying here as well. The thing standing between Rick and the Lord are things that offend Him. That's why He said, "I've overlooked them in the past but not anymore." Now that the book is open and the mystery revealed, the handwriting is easy to read. But it's up to the one who reads it to turn a new page or close the book. The choice belongs to the recipient, God will not force His hand. He is faithful to show us what offends Him to bring us to repentance. Then we can enter the fullness of our destiny in Him.

What we got away with in the past we can't get away with now. As we mature in our spiritual walk, we need to put our offenses behind us. I'm talking about being offended with other people and things that stand as an offense in our relationship to the Lord Almighty. Although I commend my brother for wanting to keep people happy and joyful, it's an offense to God when he uses vulgar overtones. And cigarettes? Personally, I don't feel they glorify the Lord in any fashion, plus they ruin your health and are outrageously expensive. I remember when I was a young girl a preacher said if God wanted you to smoke, He would have built you with a smokestack! I do believe that God is faithful to remove our desire for addictive vices if we ask Him from a sincere heart. Especially if He has shown us what we need to be delivered from He is faithful to perform His word.

My brother was given a glimpse of the other side of the fence. He could see that everything was beautiful there, vibrant in color and that's where the Lord stands with an open invitation for him to come. The Lord wants to show Rick what lies beyond. It's a choice Rick must make. I'm happy to say I have not heard one dirty joke from my brother since that day. And he has cut down tremendously with his cigarettes. I believe he will soon overcome the cigarette addiction and then he will see and know what lies beyond the fence.

I believe we all have vices, some worse than others. In the previous dream where I was thrown over the fence, I immediately repented. Then I was able to move on to my ministry. An offense will keep you gridlocked, and unable to move forward. Rick told me that after he heard the still small voice speak to him, he repented immediately about telling dirty jokes. He asked God to help him not to repeat any. And He's asked God to help him get free from the cigarette addiction. I'm very proud of the progress my brother has made.

Repentance

On the Day of Atonement, I asked the Lord what was on His heart and how could I pray? This was His response.

"Repentance Bonnie, it lies heavily upon My heart." Why you ask? "Mankind has forgotten how to repent, and others feel there's no need, grace covers it. Neither is true. My grace covers their ability to repent, conviction causes the soul to know there is a need. But true repentance comes from the heart by knowing good from evil. That a wrong has been committed and there is a need for repentance. Then, in true repentance, the person turns from it never to return to it. Why? Their love for Me is greater than their temptation to participate in it.

People's minds have been seared by the pulpit, led to think once they have been born again, they never need to repent again. That is not true. They still fall short of My glory and Holy Spirit convicts them, but they override His authority. He is the grace package within them, but they choose to follow their heart, not His leading.

This is my understanding of what He just spoke.

**When we sin Holy Spirit gives us, (the redeemed soul) conviction of our sin. This is the grace for us to repent and be forgiven of our sin we just committed.

**Sin was forgiven at the cross, for all mankind before the foundation of the world. Technically we were forgiven before we were ever born. So, any sin we would commit was already forgiven, however that was the eternal realm. In the natural we had to go through the birth process and mature. When we came to the knowledge of our sinful nature and the fact that we need a Savior, we were born again, and our sin was forgiven in the natural realm.

**Now if we sin, we must repent. Holy Spirit convicts us of our sin nature and we in turn repent.

Then the Lord said, "So, you must begin to make it very clear, repentance is still and always will be necessary. Every time you are convicted, repent, and turn from it. Keep a short list, there is little time. Time is at hand. Put your hand out in front of you now. (I stopped writing and did the activation. Putting my hands out in front of myself.) He said, "I'm at arm's length. You can reach out and touch Me." As I reached out with my hands, I could feel His presence and knew that He is always with me, ready to hear my prayers and forgive my sin. But I need to come to Him first. It's always better to repent when I'm first convicted. Why? Because if I let it linger, I'll begin to justify the sin in my mind instead of asking forgiveness. And that's where we fall into the enemy's trap. The battle begins in the mind however, Holy Spirit is ever present in our spirit. We need to listen to the still small voice and respond quickly instead of entertaining our thoughts and justifying our actions.

"He who has an ear, let him hear what the Spirit says to the churches."

Let me reinforce what I said from the beginning of this chapter. God is speaking to His children, not just the prophets and apostles. He's speaking to everyone who has an ear to hear. In Revelation chapter 2 and 3, He speaks these words to each of the seven churches. We are living in the last days of the church age, and we must pay attention to what the Spirit is saying.

The body of Christ is called to be more than conquerors and overcomers. Therefore, when He speaks and we obey, we overcome different areas in our life that have held us in bondage. We take authority over the works of Satan that have restricted us from moving according to His Spirit. To the seven churches of Revelation, He points out their qualities as well as their flaws. He ends each revelation with the same quote, "He who has an ear to hear let him hear what the Spirit says to the churches." Today we are the temple of God, the temple not built with hands. Therefore, we must listen to what the Spirit is saying. We must hear and obey. There is no other way.

Summary

2024 will be a year unlike anything we've experienced in the past. Not only are doors of opportunity open, but they are open wide! The invitation is available for all who have an ear to hear. For the remnant has gone through the fire, walked through gates of repentance, and overcome offenses. Now they're invited to come up to the Father (Revelation 4:1) where He will show them what is about to take place in the history of mankind. In this season the extraordinary will become the ordinary, the supernatural will become the natural.

After these things I looked, and behold, a door standing open in heaven. And the first voice which I heard was like a trumpet speaking with me, saying, "Come up here, and I will show you things which must take place after this." **(Revelation 4:1)**

This is not limited to a few individuals; the invitation is open for the body of believers who are ready to wield their fiery sword of power. "Excalibur" will be pulled from the Rock of Ages this year. It's the Sword of the Spirit and the Word is now more powerful than ever before because true believers are walking in power and glory.

Get ready as women move to the forefront this year in boldness and power like Peter on the day of Pentecost. Be ready to hear what the Spirit says to the seven churches of Revelation as the bride awakens to her first love and transcends time. Get ready for the open book of Revelation as the Spirit and the Bride say come!

Made in the USA
Columbia, SC
19 December 2023